DAUMIER

LIBERATED
WOMEN

DAUMIER
LIBERATED WOMEN
Bluestockings and Socialists

CATALOGUE AND CAPTIONS BY
JACQUELINE ARMINGEAT

TRANSLATED BY
SUSAN D. RESNICK

Alpine Fine Arts Collection (UK) Ltd.
Publishers of Fine Art Books, London

This book published by:
Alpine Fine Arts Collection (UK) Ltd.
43, Manchester Street
London W1M 5PE
United Kingdom
ISBN 0-88168-215-2
Printed and bound in Singapore
for Panamex (UK) Ltd., Chobham, England

Bluestockings (1844)
and Socialist Women (1849)

It's quite possible that the issue of feminism was never so forcefully stated in France as it was at the end of the 1840s, when French women tried to liberate themselves through either writing or politics. Daumier, a tried and true Republican with a liberal and open mind, was a witness to the feminist movement, but he was totally insensitive to what the women of his time strived for. It is rather surprising to see the extent to which he misunderstood women's justifiable desire for emancipation.

In his drawings Daumier mocked the women who sought equality with men, with a mercilessness that matched his exceptional talent. He ridiculed both the Bluestockings (in the series *Les Bas-bleu*), who devoted themselves to literature in 1844, and the Socialist women (*Les Femmes socialistes*), who devoted themselves to politics after the Revolution of 1848. The same themes can be found in both series of drawings: women who rebel against their husbands, who refuse to do housework and care for their children, and who give up their children to their husband's care. In each situation he portrayed the women in a state of physical disgrace.

For this reason we are presenting Daumier's lithographs in each of the two series according to their respective themes, rather than in the chronological order in which they appeared in *Le Charivari*.

Commentary on the lithographs included in this volume easily invites comparison with works of other artists such as Gavarni, and with texts of the period, including those in *Le Charivari*. There is also the text of *Le Physiologie du bas-bleu,* "Physiology of the Bluestocking" (1841-42), which immediately preceded Daumier's series in *Le Charivari* and is known to have influenced him. The two well-known novels by Balzac, *Beatrix* and *La Muse du département,* "The Regional Muse" (1843), deal with the failure of the "superior woman." There is also Flaubert's *L'Éducation Sentimentale,* "A Sentimental Education" (1843), and his correspondence with Louise Colet, as well as allusions to women writers and famous Socialist women, including the writings of Louise Colet.

–Voyez-donc un peu, Isménie !.... comment le Gouvernement permet-il
d'afficher de pareilles turpitudes?...

C'est singulier comme ce miroir m'applatit la taille et me maigrit la poitrine que m'importe?... Mme de Staël et Mr de Buffon l'ont proclamé... **le génie n'a point de sexe**.

L'artiste m'a représenté au moment ou j'écris mon sombre volume intitulé **vapeurs de mon âme!**...l'œil n'est pas mal, mais le nez ne me semble pas suffisamment affligé!....

(Le monsieur à part) — Oui.....il n'est qu'affligeant.....

— Adieu ma chère Flora..... ne manquez pas d'adresser au bureau du journal deux exemplaires de vos **bulles de savon**... et je ferai mousser cela dans mon feuilleton.

— Messieurs, je viens offrir à votre journal, un roman-feuilleton qui je crois lui conviendra parfaitement!.. il a pour titre **Eloa ou huit jours de bonheur intime**... la première partie formera dix ou douze volumes.... à la manière d'Eugène Sue!....

— Pardon madame!.. mais ceci me parait effrayant... à ce compte là vos **huit jours** dureront trois ans!..

Nos comptes sont faciles à établir... vous m'aviez confié mille exemplaires de votre recueil poétique intitulé **soupirs de mon âme**... vingt sept volumes ont été donnés aux journaux... et en défalquant ce que j'ai vendu je trouve qu'il me reste juste neuf cent soixante treize **soupirs de votre âme** dans mon magasin!....

—Monsieur, pardon si je vous gêne un peu . . . . mais vous comprenez qu'écrivant en ce moment un roman nouveau, je dois consulter une foule d'auteurs anciens ! . . . . . .

— (Le Monsieur à part.) des auteurs anciens ! . . . . parbleu elle aurait bien du les consulter de leur vivant, car elle a du être leur contemporaine ! . . . .

(*Le parterre de l'Odéon*.) — L'auteur! .. l'auteur! .. l'auteur! . . .
—Messieurs, votre impatience va être satisfaite . . . vous désirez connaître l'auteur de l'ouvrage remarquable qui vient d'obtenir un si grand, et je dois le dire, si légitime succès . . . . cet auteur . . . . c'est môa!

Le bas bas bleu déclamant sa pièce. — Acte sixieme, premier tableau... le théatre représente un tigre endormi dans le désert.... Rosalba s'avance en se trainant avec peine et en trainant avec plus de peine encore ses cinq enfans et son vieux père; — Rosalba tombe au pied d'un dattier couvert de noix de cocos et s'ecrie avec désespoir !.... Ô ciel quand finiront nos tourmens !....

Tous les auditeurs (A voix basse) et les notres quand donc finiront ils ô ciel !.....

Enfer et damnation!.. siflée!....siflée!!.... siiiflée!!...

Allons !... on n'a pas encore rendu compte de mon roman aujourd'hui ! ces journalistes s'occupent maintenant tous les matins des Lièvres..... des Perdreaux.... des Bécasses !.... et ils ne pensent pas a moi... c'est inconcevable !....

Ce Journal trouve mon ouvrage pitoyable.... cette fois encore je suis donc incomprise!

Ah vous trouvez que mon dernier roman n'est pas tout-à-fait à la hauteur de ceux de Georges Sand....! Adélaïde, je ne vous reverrai de la vie!

Adieu Ophélia!... ne manquez pas de venir mardi soir.... c'est une réunion littéraire en petit comité.... nous lirons des élégies et nous ferons du bischoff!...

— Suivez-bien mon raisonnement, Eudoxie... tout doit tendre à un but humanitaire, en conséquence chaque ligne que nous écrivons doit procéder de l'analyse pour arriver à la synthèse... sans quoi le socialisme n'est plus que de l'égoïsme... engendrant le matérialisme et... vous offrirai-je encore une tasse de thé ?....

LA PRÉSIDENTE CRIANT À TUE TÊTE.

Mesdames!.. vous violez formellement l'article trois de notre règlement... le quel porte que les aca-demiciennes ne parleront jamais plus de cinq à la fois!.. je vous rappelle toutes à l'ordre.... et au silence!.. puisque ma sonnette est impuissante.... je lève la séance et je mets mon chapeau!.. jettez maintenant tant que vous voudrez vos bonnets par dessus les moulins!.....

Nous voilà donc réunies pour écrire le premier numéro de notre journal . . . Le Sans Culotte
– littéraire . . . . qu'est-ce nous allons commencer par échiner ? . . . .
– Pour commencer . . . . échignons tout ! . . . . .

– Madame, comment trouvez-vous cette cigarette?...

– C'est bien fadasse .... et bon tout au plus pour des femmes d'agens de change en goguette!.. quant à moi je n'aime que les plus gros cigarres du plus Gros-Caillou possible ... du reste je compose en ce moment un sonnet sur le tabac caporal .... je le publierai dans un volume intitulé fumées de ma pipe.

Ô plaisir de l'opium que tu me ravis!.. il me semble que j'habite l'orient.... du reste je ne sais quelle voix secrète me criait depuis longtemps que ma véritable patrie aurait du être le désert!

Femme de lettre humanitaire se livrant sur l'homme a des réflexions crânement philosophiques !

O Lune!... inspire moi ce soir quelque petite pensée un peu grandiose!... car je t'aime ainsi, lorsque tu me présentes en entier la face pâle et mélancolique!.... mais, ô Lune, je t'affectionne moins lorsque tu m'apparais sous la forme d'un croissant....parceque alors tu me rappelles tout bonnement mon mari!...

— Dis donc Bichette...à quoi songes tu donc de te promener comme ça la nuit ?... est-ce que t'es somnambule, où bien, est-ce que t'as la colique ?...

— Non...je cherche un moyen neuf de tuer un mari....je ne me recouche pas que je n'ai trouvé mon moyen!...il me le faut pour terminer mon roman!...

— Saperlotte!...pourvu qu'elle ne l'assaye pas sur moi!....

Dire qu'Arsinoé n'était pas contente d'être portraiturée, Daguerréotypée, lithographiée et biographiée!.... il faut maintenant que je paie trois mille francs pour son buste en marbre... c'est dur!.... pour comble de malheur me voilà obligé d'épousseter ma femme tous les matins ....et c'est qu'elle en fait de la poussière ma femme !....

Saperlotte !... que je voudrais donc que ma femme ait fini d'improviser son quatrain sur **les beautés de la nature dans la plaine** S.t **Denis**....! nous marchons toujours, mais ses vers n'avancent pas !....

O douleur !... avoir rêvé pendant toute ma vie de jeune fille un époux, qui, ainsi que moi, adorât la sainte poésie, et tomber sur un mari qui n'aime que les goujons..... cet homme-là était né pour être brochet !.....

— O mon Victor idolatré.....il me vient une idée poétique !! précipitons nous ensemble et a l'instant du haut de cette grise falaise dans les flots bleus de l'Océan !.....

— Nous noyer dans la mer !...nous y réfléchirons, Anastasie,....je tiens à descendre encore pendant quelque temps le fleuve de la vie !...

Allons bon !.. la v'là qui au lieu de lait, verse du cirage dans mon chocolat !......
satané roman va !...

Depuis que Virginie a obtenu la septième accessit de poesie a l'academie française il faut que ce soit moi.... moi capitaine de la garde nationale.... qui compte tous les samedis le linge a donner a la blanchisseuse... et je le fais parceque sans cela ma femme me laverait la tête!...

— Bichette . . . viens donc arranger ma rosette ! . . . .

— Voila bien les hommes ! . . . comme ils abusent de leurs droits parce qu'on a eu un jour la foiblesse de serrer avec eux les nœuds de l'hymenée, ils voudraient ensuite vous faire serrer a perpétuité ceux de leurs cravattes ! . . mais je suis décidée a suivre désormais les principes émis ce matin même par **Artémise Jabutot** dans son remarquable article de la **Gazette des femmes libres** : . . . a bas les nœuds de cravattes et les boutons de pantalons !

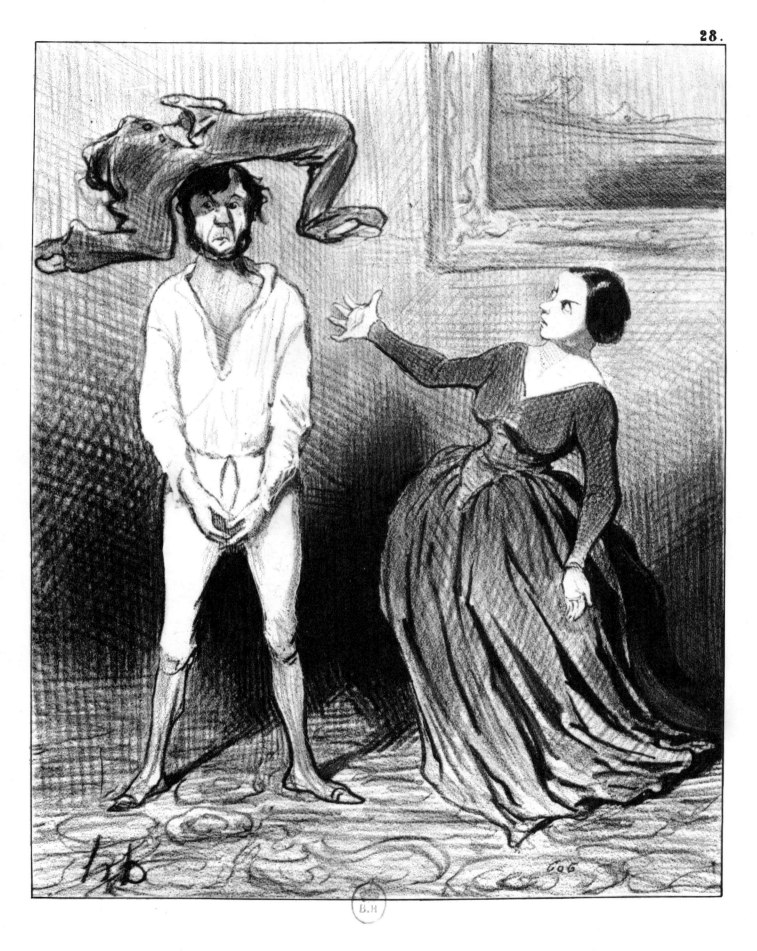

Une femme comme moi ... remettre un bouton? ... vous êtes fou! ....
Allons bon! .. voila qu'elle ne se contente plus de porter les culottes .... il faut encore
qu'elle me les jette à là tête! ....

La mère est dans le feu de la composition, l'enfant est dans l'eau de la baignoire !

Emportez donc ça plus loin... il est impossible de travailler au milieu d'un vacarme pareil... allez vous promener à la petite provence, et en revenant, achetez de nouveaux biberons passage Choiseul !... Ah! Mr Cabassol c'est votre premier enfant, mais je vous jure que ce sera votre dernier!

— Satané piallard d'enfant va!.... laisse moi donc composer en paix mon ode sur le bonheur de la maternité!....

— C'est bon, c'est bon,....il va se taire....je vais aller lui donner le fouet dans l'autre pièce....
(à part.) dans le fait de tous les ouvrages de ma femme c'est bien celui qui fait le plus de bruit dans le monde!....

Adieu mon cher, je vais chez mes éditeurs, ...je ne rentrerai probablement que fort tard... ne manquez pas de donner encore deux fois la bouillie à Dodore .... s'il a besoin..... d'autre chose .... vous trouverez ça sous le lit ....

— Ma bonne amie, puis-je entrer !.... as-tu fini de collaborer avec monsieur ?......

Dis donc... mon mari... j'ai bien envie d'appeler mon drame **Arthur** et d'intituler mon enfant **Oscar**!.. mais non... toute réflexion faite, je ne deciderai rien avant d'avoir consulté mon collaborateur!....

— C'est singulier... il ne me vient plus d'idées maintenant que lorsque je suis au bois de Boulogne et que je trotte avec M. Edouard !...

— Quelles idées peuvent donc venir à ma femme, quand elle trotte avec M. Edouard ?.... ceci m'intrigue... je suis faché de voir qu'elle s'est faite amazone... j'aurais mieux aimé qu'elle restât simplement à cheval sur la vertu !...

Ah! ma chère, quelle singulière éducation vous donnez à votre fille?... mais à douze ans, moi, j'avais déja écrit un roman en deux volumes . et même une fois terminé, ma mère m'avait défendu de le lire, tellement elle le trouvait avancé pour mon âge...

........................dussent-ils me maudire »

« Ces barbares parens qui m'ont donné le jour, »

« Ô Victor, ô mon âme, a toi tout mon amour ! »

– Bravo....bravo....bravo....qu'une mère est heureuse d'avoir une petite fille pareille!...

Comment! encore une caricature sur nous, ce matin, dans le **Charivari** !... ah! jour de ma vie! j'espère bien que cette fois c'est la dernière!... et si jamais ce Daumier me tombe sous la main, il lui en coutera cher pour s'etre permis de tricoter des **Bas bleus**.

L'insurrection contre les maris est proclamée le plus saint des devoirs !

— Ah! il prétend m'empêcher d'aller communier avec nos huit cents frères à la barrière du Maine.....
il faut que je punisse tant d'insolence!
— Arrêtez, Eglantine, laissez ce tyran aux remords de sa conscience.

—Ah! vous êtes mon mari, ah! vous êtes le maître . . . . . . eh! bien moi, j'ai le droit de vous flanquer à la porte de chez vous . . . . . Jeanne Derouin me l'a prouvé hier soir ! . . . . allez vous expliquer avec elle! . . . .

— Oui, ma chère, mon mari a ravalé ma dignité de femme jusqu'à me forcer ce matin a recoudre un bouton de bretelle!........
— Jour de ma vie, si un homme me forçait à travailler à sa culotte!......

— Comme vous vous faites belle, ma chère ?....

— Ah! c'est que je vais a un banquet présidé par Pierre Leroux,......et si vous saviez comme il est vétilleux pour la toilette !......

— Ma femme reste bien long-temps à ce banquet ...... voilà bientôt quarante huit heures qu'elle est partie !

— Il parait que les clubs vont être complétement fermés . . . . . .
— Les **réacs** . . . . . ils n'auraient jamais osé faire cela avant que la légion des **Vésuviennes**
fut dissoute ! . . . . .

LES FEMMES SOCIALISTES.

.........qu'est la femme aujourd'hui dans la société, rien! que doit-elle être tout..... oui, tout, tout !.....
— Ah! bravo, bravo, c'est encore plus beau que le dernier discours de Jeanne Derouin!.....

« Les délégués du club **central socialiste** ont à l'unanimité repoussé la candidature de Jeanne Derouin! »
—Oh! les aristos!....

— Repoussée comme candidate à l'assemblée nationale, une porte me reste encore ouverte.........
laisse moi Zénobie....... ne trouble pas mes pensées......je suis en train de rédiger un manifeste
à l'Europe!.......

Catalogue

BLUESTOCKINGS.

A series of forty plates, numbered from 1 to 40 and published in *Le Charivari* from January to August 1844. L. Delteil, 1221 to 1260.

Littre defines *Bluestocking* as: "The pejorative name given to women who, in busying themselves with literature, brought a certain pedantry to it." According to Esquiros ("Revue des deux mondes," April 1860, p. 778, quoted by Littre), the expression *Bluestocking* comes from England ("blue-stocking"). Mrs. Stillingfleet, one of the members of a literary club that gathered at the home of Mrs. Montagu around 1781, always wore blue stockings. "Her conversation was so excellent that whenever she was absent, it became customary to say: 'We can't do anything tonight without the Blue stockings.' Little by little clubs were founded under the same name. Eventually the term 'Bluestocking' was extended to refer to women of letters who were either pedantic or ridiculous."

1. — ISMENIE! TAKE A LOOK AT THIS! . . . HOW CAN THE GOVERNMENT ALLOW THE POSTING OF SUCH BLASPHE-MIES? . . .

L. Delteil, 1260, second of three artist's proofs. Plate 40 and last of the series. Published in *Le Charivari*, August 7, 1844.

"In France, all women have minds, except for the Bluestock-ings" (Madame de Girardin). Some of Daumier's plates were inspired by *Le Physiologie du bas-bleu*, "Physiology of the Bluestocking",(1841-42, by Frederic Soulie, vignettes by Jules Vernier). The eccentricities of what Molière called "knowl-edgeable women" are described with the same point of view. Soulie says that he likes the expression "Bluestocking," offering as explanation only that "[it denounces] that type of woman with a word of the masculine gender" (in French: *le* bas-bleu).

Gavarni directed numerous jibes at the Bluestockings, a fact alluded to in the Goncourt's *Journal* (1853, 1:116), which recounted that the artist often made fun of the Bluestockings in the social milieu in which he lived— "Lyricism and stew. It smelled of cabbage."— and criticized their unbelievable way of dressing. The theater also poked fun at the Bluestockings. A vaudeville act by Ferdinand Langle and F. Devilleneuve, *The Bluestockings,* was created at the Variétés Theater on January 24, 1842.

Le Charivari of course took ample opportunity to satirize the Bluestockings in its chronicles: "We know the British Bluestock-ings. They're the leaders, the fathers of them all. The German Bluestockings are a very close second for the oldness of the British ones. The origins of the Italian Bluestockings are lost in the dark ages. Those in Sweden were invented by Sweden-bourg and Mr. Balzac. Finally came the French Bluestockings, already described many times and sufficiently known by the naturalists . . ." (June 7, 1849).

2. — IT'S REMARKABLE HOW THIS MIRROR MAKES MY WAIST THINNER AND MY BUST FLATTER. SO WHAT? . . . AS MADAME DE STAËL AND MONSIEUR DE BUFFON PRO-CLAIMED "GENIUS HAS NO GENDER!"

L. Delteil, 1221, second of three artist's proofs. Plate 1 of the series. Published in *Le Charivari*, June 30, 1844.

"Someone telling me that a woman has a mind and intelli-gence is not what I want to know. Is she pretty? That's all I ask that a woman be" (Fontenelle). For Daumier, a woman with pretensions to "genius" negates her sex and is thus deprived of her charm. The theme of physical disgrace associated with the Bluestockings is present in almost all the plates in the series. Moreover, Daumier almost never drew young and graceful women. "Above all he needed the traces of experience that life imprints on people: wrinkles, jowls, sagging flesh, dried out chins . . . from this he drew his terrible shrews and gossips" (Duranty, *Gazette des beaux arts,* 1878). It must be added that Daumier's men were not treated any better.

Physiology of the Bluestocking portrayed the kind of woman born under the Restoration: "Every Bluestocking of the time thought she was the accomplice of Madame de Staël, and like her made herself a victim of the Emperor." Napoleon had said to Madame de Staël: "The leading lady of the world is she who makes the most children."

3. — THE ARTIST PORTRAYED ME AS I WAS WRITING MY SOMBER VOLUME TITLED *Vapors of My Soul!* . . . THE EYE ISN'T BAD, BUT THE NOSE DOESN'T SEEM SUFFICIENTLY AFFLICTED! . . .

— [THE UNSEEN GENTLEMEN:] HMM . . . IT'S NOTHING BUT AFFLICTING . . .

L. Delteil, 1243, second of three artist's proofs. Plate 23 of the series. Published in *Le Charivari*, April 15, 1844.

In this very ugly woman author, Philippe Roberts-Jones sees "a very ungracious type of woman reproduced in six different lithographs: a very thin woman whose face resembles the head of a lamb. The aquiline nose prolongs the curve of the forehead. The eyes are large and bulging. The mouth is puckered and the chin straight" (*Études de quelques types physionomiques dans l'oeuvre de Daumier*, "Study of Certain Types of Physiognomies in the Work of Daumier," Brussels, 1949). One of the six other lithographs in question is part of the Bluestockings series.

4. — GOOD-BYE MY DEAR FLORA . . . DON'T FORGET TO SEND TWO COPIES OF YOUR "SOAP BUBBLES" TO THE NEWSPAPER OFFICE . . .

— I'LL WHIP IT UP INTO MY LITERARY ARTICLE.

L. Delteil, 1241, second of three artist's proofs. Plate 21 of the series. Published in *Le Charivari*, April 6, 1844.

Daumier retained only the mediocre or ridiculous aspect of women's literature at the beginning of the nineteenth century. It's true that the kinds of things women were publishing at that time were very inconsistent. Francis Jourdain recounts in the same spirit how his grandmother, Madame Laure Jourdain, a writer of lyrics, rhymed *dieux et cieux*, "Gods and Heavens," and *abandons et pardons*, "relinquishment and forgiveness." Among the women poets and their works published during this period were Elisa Fleury (a weaver), *La Lice chansonnière*, "Song List"; Elise Moreau (a peasant from the town of Deux-Sèvres, *Rêves d'une jeune fille*, "Dreams of a Young Girl" (1837); Marie Carpentier de la Flèche, *Préludes*; Marie-Laure from Normandy, *Églantines*; and Marceline Desbordes-Valmore, *Les Pleurs*, "Tears" (1833), and *Pauvres Fleurs*, "Poor Flowers" (1839).

There was another literature as well during this time, although Daumier pretended to ignore it. The novels of Madame de Staël were of considerable influence: *Delphine* (1802), and especially *Corinne* (1807), became a symbol. Women who "believed themselves to be out of the ordinary imagined that they were like Corinne" (*Almanac des dames*, "Ladies' Almanac," 1807). A Delphine or a Corinne "is always a woman of superior gifts, who is unable to limit herself to the role that public opinion has designated for her in life, and thus, before long she falls prey to the cruelest agonies because she has wandered from her assigned line of conduct," wrote Madame Necker de Saussure in her work on Madame de Staël. George Sand made a major contribution toward developing the idea of women's liberation in her novels *Spiridion* (1838), *Compagnon du tour de France*, "Companion Through France" (1840), *Indiana*, and *Consuelo*.

The character of the "woman author" was of great interest to Balzac. In *Beatrix* (1838), he portrayed "an exceptional woman" who had "an uncanny facility in conceiving and understanding everything; she could discuss metaphysics and music, theology and painting . . . But there was a bit of an affectation about her; she seemed to know too many difficult things, like Chinese and Hebrew. She had doubts about the hieroglyphics and was able to explain the nature of the papyrus that envelops the Egyptian mummies." In *La Muse du département*, "The Regional Muse" (1843), Balzac told the story of Dinah de la Baudraye, who "thirsty for knowledge," tried to "form a literary society," and who followed "the counsel of the good abbot Duret who told her to convert her bad thoughts into poetry, . . . Heartache is appeased, as the alexandrines bubble in the brain." However, after she had written a long poem, Duret told her: "Don't write anything else, . . . or you will no longer be a woman. You will be a poet."

Flaubert did not share this opinion. He wrote to Louise Colet, with whom he had a long relationship, that he didn't find her "superficial and insipid like other women." In a letter dated Saturday, August 8, 1846, he told her: "Tomorrow I'm waiting to read your verses, and in a few days your two volumes." And then ". . . Yes, work hard and love Art" (August 9, 1846), and "Work, write something for me that's grand, somber, beautiful and severe, . . . so that I can be proud of it . . ." (September 15, 1846). Laure, Balzac's sister, would also become a writer.

5. — GENTLEMEN, I'VE COME TO OFFER YOU A SERIAL NOVEL THAT I BELIEVE IS PERFECT FOR YOUR NEWSPAPER . . . IT'S TITLED *Eloa, or Eight Days of Intimate Happiness* . . . THE FIRST PART WILL CONSTITUTE TEN OR TWELVE ISSUES . . . IN THE MANNER OF EUGENE SUE! . . .

— I BEG YOUR PARDON, MADAM! . . . BUT THIS IS A FRIGHTENING PROSPECT . . . AT THAT RATE YOUR "EIGHT DAYS" WILL LAST THREE YEARS!

L. Delteil, 1226, second of three artist's proofs (before final for "Bluestockings"). Plate 6 of the series. Published in *Le Charivari*, February 13, 1844.

"A Bluestocking rarely makes what we refer to as a 'social call' except when it's to solicit the placement of a manuscript that is, according to the circumstances, her first hope or her last chance" (*Physiology of the Bluestocking*). According to the same work, the "real Bluestocking" is characterized by "a thin body that floats somewhere in between forty and forty-five years of age." Stendhal advised: "A woman should only start writing at the age of fifty. Publishing is dangerous, because she could risk losing her lover."

6. — IT'S EASY TO BALANCE OUR ACCOUNT . . . YOU DELIVERED ONE THOUSAND COPIES OF YOUR COLLECTED POEMS TITLED SIGHS FROM MY SOUL . . . TWENTY-SEVEN BOOKS WERE GIVEN TO THE NEWSPAPERS . . . AND IN DEDUCTING WHAT I'VE SOLD I FIND THAT I HAVE EXACTLY NINE HUNDRED SEVENTY-THREE "SIGHS FROM YOUR SOUL" LEFT IN MY STORE! . . .

L. Delteil, 1250, third of three artist's proofs. Plate 30 of the series. Published in *Le Charivari*, June 17, 1844.

Théophile Gautier was more indulgent with regard to women authors: "After all, what difference does it make if women scribble on some sheets of paper? Is it so necessary that men maintain the monopoly on writing nonsense? As for us, we like a woman who writes, a Bluestocking, just as much as we like a woman who plays piano and studies the more or less impossible variations of Hertz all day long."

7. — Excuse me, sir, for disturbing you a bit ... but you can understand how it is ... I'm writing a new novel now, and I've got to consult so many ancient authors! ...

— [The gentleman to himself:] Ancient authors! ... of course! She should have consulted them while they were living, since she must have been their contemporary! ...

L. Delteil, 1233, second of three artist's proofs. Plate 13 of the series. Published in *Le Charivari*, March 8, 1844.

Eugénie Niboyet, of whom we will speak at greater length with *Les Femmes socialistes*, dealt with education for women, the area in which she concentrated her efforts. In particular, she asked that a reading room for women be opened at the Bibliothèque Nationale.

8. The box at the Odeon Theater in Paris

— The Author! ... Author! ... Author! ...

— Gentlemen, your impatience is about to be satisfied ... You want to know the author of the remarkable play that has just obtained such a great, and, if I must say, legitimate success ... That author ... is meee!

L. Delteil, 1237, second of three artist's proofs. Plate 17 of the series. Published in *Le Charivari*, March 17, 1844.

"Famous women have a vague resemblance to men. They have neither the flexibility nor the abandon that women who nature destined for maternity have" (Balzac, *Beatrix*). "Not being born a man is the greatest regret of a Parisian woman" (Taxile Delord, *Physiologie de la Parisienne*, "Physiology of the Parisian Woman," vignettes by Menut-Alophe, 1841-42).

9. The Bluestocking reads her play.

— Act Six, Scene One ... The theater presents on stage a tiger asleep in the desert ... Rosalba moves forward with difficulty as she pulls along with even more difficulty her five children and her old father.

— Rosalba falls at the foot of a palm tree covered with coconuts and cries out in despair! ... Heavens, when will this torment end! ...

— [All the people listening, with lowered voices:] —And when will our torment end, oh heavens!

L. Delteil, 1242, second of three artist's proofs. Plate 22 of the series. Published in *Le Charivari*, April 10, 1844.

"I've always been turned off by a woman with grand airs, the woman writer or artist; how even the most educated, including the most illustrious among them, have always seemed to me so lacking in genius, ... while the working woman ... has my homage and my attachment" (Proudhon, letter to his fiancée, 1847). Proudhon wrote in 1849: "At the age of forty-one, I married a simple Parisian work woman ... who is as little a Bluestocking as she is a 'cordon bleu' cook." He didn't realize that she had suffered and always would suffer from a lack of education. Proudhon's position was completely antifeminist: for him women could only be "housewives or courtesans," completely bereft of social distinction. Such blatant antifeminism is rather strange to see in a Socialist.

Daumier's antifeminism also targeted literary salons. "Seeing herself listened to with ecstasy, she gradually got used to listening to herself, as well, and began to take pleasure in spouting out, ultimately considering her friends as confidantes in a tragedy who were destined to provide her with cues" (Balzac).

10. — Hell and damnation! ... hiss! ... hiss!! ... hissssssss!! ...

L. Delteil, 1239, third of three artist's proofs. Plate 19 of the series. Published in *Le Charivari*, March 24, 1844.

This plate along with the three that follow shows the despair, surprise, annoyance, or wrath of the woman author whose work has not been appreciated. She deems herself misunderstood and shunned. (The piece that was "hissed" must have been a somber drama, judging by the sword Daumier had the cruel irony to point in the author's direction.)

11. — My, my! They didn't even review my novel in today's paper! These journalists spend their time writing about rabbits ... partridges ... geese! ... and they don't write about me ... That's inconceivable!

L. Delteil, 1230, second of three artist's proofs. Plate 10 of the series. Published in *Le Charivari*, February 25, 1844.

Facing criticism and ridicule, this Bluestocking came to have dinner in a restaurant with an essentially male clientele. Their expression shows surprise tinged with mockery. Is it merely her presence that mystifies them, or is it her attire? "When they're old, these women are ridiculously decked out in their bonnets like packhorses at mid-Lent; they're swimming in waves of ribbons. A Bluestocking doesn't know how to choose a hat at any age" (*Physiology of the Bluestocking*).

12. — This newspaper finds my work pitiful ... Again I've been misunderstood! ...

L. Delteil, 1258, second of two artist's proofs. Plate 38 of the series. Published in *Le Charivari*, August 1, 1844.

"The day a cook can believe in the superiority of her mistress is a more glorious day for a Bluestocking than the day they crown her at the Capitol." Unfortunately for the latter, there is no glory; she's "misunderstood."

Even her cook looks quizzical. Her physical portrayal bears a strange resemblance to the description given in *Physiology of the Bluestocking:* " ... diaphanous hands, humped feet, carefully neglected black hair, cavernous eyes racked by tears."

13. — I see! You think my most recent novel isn't quite up to those of George Sand! ... Well, Adelaide, I never in my life want to see you again!

L. Delteil, 1254, second of two artist's proofs. Plate 34 of the series. Published in *Le Charivari*, July 18, 1844.

It's one thing to be misunderstood by men, but to be misunderstood by another woman is the ultimate injustice. At least she can console herself with a phrase by Balzac, whose Madame de la Baudraye is told by the king's procurator, "You're much too superior a woman for other women to like you" (*The Regional Muse*).

14. — FAREWELL, OPHELIA! . . . DON'T FORGET TO COME ON TUESDAY EVENING . . . IT'S A SMALL LITERARY GATHERING . . . WE'RE GOING TO READ ELEGIES AND MAKE MULLED WINE! . . .

L. Delteil, 1224, second of three artist's proofs (*Adieu* instead of *Au revoir* in the third artist's proof). Plate 4 of the series. Published in *Le Charivari*, February 10, 1844.

Daumier now attacks the literary gatherings of the ladies whom he doesn't take very seriously: " . . . We'll make mulled wine!" is analogous to the situation that upsets Madame de la Baudraye when she attempts to form a literary society: "From the second year on they played dominoes, billiards, and cards, while drinking hot, sweet wine, punch, and liqueurs . . ." (Balzac, *The Regional Muse*).

Daumier, who portrayed the majority of his Bluestockings in ornately furnished bourgeois interiors, had fun with this illustration's unusual composition. The woman who's leaning on the stairwell is perhaps part of the "variety" of Bluestockings who wear severe "dresses of pearl gray," which confuses them with "British governesses. This very specific type of woman drinks water, eats bread and gruel, and never speaks to her children in a familiar tone . . ." (*Physiology of the Bluestocking*).

15. — FOLLOW MY REASONING CLOSELY, EUDOXIE . . . EVERYTHING MUST MOVE IN THE DIRECTION OF A HUMANITARIAN GOAL. CONSEQUENTLY, EVERY LINE THAT WE WRITE MUST PROCEED FROM ANALYSIS IN ORDER TO ARRIVE AT SYNTHESIS . . . WITHOUT WHICH SOCIALISM IS NOTHING MORE THAN EGOISM . . . ENGENDERING MATERIALISM AND . . . WOULD YOU LIKE ANOTHER CUP OF TEA?

L. Delteil, 1251, second of two artist's proofs. Plate 31 of the series. Published in *Le Charivari*, June 26, 1844.

After the Revolution of 1830, and under the influence of "the fame of George Sand," we see "young girls or young women distracted from a calm life by the appearance of fame! Strange doctrines were then published regarding the role of women in society . . . Women started expressing ideas and expounding sentiments that a few years earlier they never would have admitted to" (Balzac, *The Regional Muse*).

16. — [THE PRESIDENT SCREAMING AT THE TOP OF HER LUNGS:] LADIES! YOU ARE FORMALLY VIOLATING ARTICLE THREE OF OUR RULES AND REGULATIONS . . . WHICH SAYS THAT NO MORE THAN FIVE ACADEMICIANS WILL SPEAK AT THE SAME TIME! . . . I CALL YOU ALL TO ORDER . . . AND SILENCE! . . . SINCE MY BELL IS HAVING NO

EFFECT WHATSOEVER . . . I'M CLOSING THE MEETING AND PUTTING ON MY HAT! . . . NOW YOU CAN FLING YOUR BONNETS INTO THE WIND FOR ALL I CARE!

L. Delteil, 1245, second of two artist's proofs. Plate 25 of the series. Published in *Le Charivari*, April 24, 1844.

Daumier rendered the tumult of this women's meeting with talent and adeptness. *Le Charivari* didn't control its sarcasm either when dealing with the pretentiousness of women wanting to meet among themselves, and published in the June 7, 1849, issue a chronicle titled *Une fausse alarme*, "A False Alarm," that exposed how the women of Grenada "asked the government to reserve one of the rooms of the Alhambra for their use . . . in order to establish an academy where only women would be admitted."

Masson's caricature titled *Club des femmes*, "The Women's Club" (1848), includes this caption: "All that I can grant you is that only twenty-five at a time will talk!" (Bibliothèque Nationale, the Vinck Print Collection). The gatherings of the Bluestockings were the forerunners of the "women's clubs" that came into being after the Revolution of 1848 (see *Socialist Women*, No. 47). Arago writes to Garnier-Pages: "Our meetings are cluttered with a troupe of shrews that make them unbearable with their strained exclamations and their absurd demands."

17. — HERE WE ARE TO WRITE THE FIRST VOLUME OF OUR NEWSPAPER, *The Extreme Literary Republican* . . . WHAT SHALL WE KNOCK OFF FIRST? . . .

— TO START WITH . . . LET'S KNOCK THE WHOLE THING OFF! . . .

L. Delteil, 1253, second of two artist's proofs. Plate 33 of the series. Published in *Le Charivari*, July 14, 1844.

"Felicity remained in a chair near the window, taken up with smoking . . ." (Balzac, *Beatrix*). Men's clothing and George Sand's cigars became legendary habiliments, and certain women writers dedicated themselves to these new "occupations." One of the chapters of *Physiology of the Bluestocking* is dedicated to the "liberated Bluestocking" who "wants to be a Deputy, a Constituent, an attorney; who smokes, . . . who writes newspaper articles for papers that existed, or that will exist . . ."

18. — HOW DO YOU LIKE THAT CIGARETTE, MADAM? . . .

— IT'S QUITE INSIPID . . . AND AT BEST GOOD FOR WOMEN STOCKBROKERS OUT ON A SPREE! . . . I PREFER THE LARGEST CIGARS, THE BIGGEST "GROS-CAILLOU" AVAILABLE FROM THE TOBACCO DISTRICT . . . WHAT'S MORE, AT THE MOMENT I'M COMPOSING A SONNET ON TOBACCO . . . I'LL PUBLISH IT IN A VOLUME TITLED *Smoke from My Pipe*.

L. Delteil, 1229, second of two artist's proofs. Plate 9 of the series. Published in *Le Charivari*, March 9, 1844.

Between 1810 and 1909, a tobacco factory at 63 Quai d'Orsay in the neighborhood of Gros-Caillou manufactured not only smoking and snuffing tobaccos, but also cigars that sold for one or two pennies apiece. For the author of *Physiologie du fumeur*,

"Physiology of the Smoker" (1841), ". . . the two-bit cigar was incontestably the best." He dedicated a chapter to *La femme, faite homme,* "The Woman, Made Man," which speaks of the woman ". . . who nobly uses the right to smoke."

19. — AH, OPIUM! HOW YOU RAVISH ME WITH PLEASURE! . . . IT'S AS IF I WERE LIVING IN THE ORIENT . . . MOREOVER, I KNOW NOT WHAT SECRET VOICE HAS BEEN SCREAMING AT ME FOR SO LONG THAT MY TRUE HOME-LAND SHOULD HAVE BEEN THE DESERT!

L. Delteil, 1246, second of four artist's proofs. Plate 26 of the series. Published in *Le Charivari,* May 7, 1844.

"When she was alone, the author gave way to the woman; she broke into tears, stuffed tobacco drenched in opium into the spout of her opium pipe, and spent the major part of the night smoking . . ." (Balzac, *Beatrix*). There was also an allusion to Saint-Simon in this caricature, whose apostles waited for "the Mother" to become the head of their community. Judging that she would, like the first "Savior," issue from the east, they went with Father Enfantin to search for her in Egypt. Numerous women joined this deceptive expedition, hence the allusion to the desert.

20. A WOMAN OF HUMANE LETTERS CONTEMPLATING MAN WITH PLUCKILY PHILOSOPHIC REFLECTIONS.

L. Delteil, 1235, second of four artist's proofs. Plate 15 of the series. Published in *Le Charivari,* March 10, 1844.

With obvious satisfaction and a lot of wit Daumier dedicated numerous plates in the series to portraying the attitude of the Bluestockings toward their husbands: disdain, indifference, rebellion . . . Perhaps he, like Proudhon, thought that "liberty for women can only consist in the liberty to do housework" (*Le Peuple,* 1849). The "humanitarian" ideas of Monsieur de la Baudraye's wife had equally little appeal: "When she had taken on the issue of Negroes, or the betterment of the conditions of prisoners, he took his little blue cap and silently stole away . . ." (Balzac, *The Regional Muse*).

Daumier, who liked to play with the effects of light, used the flame of a candle (as in No. 22) to create large fantastic shadows and to accentuate the graceless traits of the "woman of humanitarian letters."

21. — OH MOON! . . . INSPIRE ME TONIGHT WITH SOME SMALL THOUGHT A LITTLE GRANDIOSE! . . . BECAUSE I LOVE YOU THUS, WHEN YOU SHOW YOUR FULL PALE AND MELANCHOLY FACE TO ME! . . . BUT, I ALSO HAVE AFFEC-TION FOR YOU WHEN YOU APPEAR BEFORE ME IN THE FORM OF A CROISSANT . . . BECAUSE THEN YOU REMIND ME OF MY HUSBAND! . . .

L. Delteil, 1228, second of three artist's proofs. Plate 8 of the series. Published in *Le Charivari,* February 28, 1844.

Eugénie de Guerin exclaims in her *Notes* (1839): "Ah yes! I've got something in my head. What must I do? My God! a tiny work in which I will frame my thoughts, my points of view . . . I'll throw myself into it, the overflowing of my life, the bubbling over of my soul . . . Where shall I aim? A goal, a

goal." Here, it's in front of a full moon that the woman author searches for inspiration. The idea of a crescent moon, symbol of the cuckolded husband, was used many times by Daumier. (See the series *Daumier: Moeurs Conjugales,* "Conjugal Manners," preface, catalogue, and notes by Philippe Roberts-Jones, ed. A. Sauret, 1967, Nos. 25 [L.D. 648] and 53 [L.D. 676].)

22. — TELL ME, BICHETTE . . . WHAT IN THE WORLD ARE YOU THINKING OF THAT MAKES YOU WALK AROUND LIKE THIS AT NIGHT? . . . ARE YOU SLEEPWALKING, OR ARE YOU HAVING AN ATTACK OF COLIC? . . .
— NO . . . I'M SEARCHING FOR A NEW WAY OF KILLING A HUSBAND . . . I'M NOT COMING BACK TO BED UNTIL I'VE FOUND MY VEHICLE! . . . I NEED IT TO FINISH MY NOVEL! . . .
— GOOD GRIEF! . . . AS LONG AS SHE DOESN'T BASE IT ON ME! . . .

L. Delteil 1225, second of four artist's proofs. Plate 5 of the series. Published in *Le Charivari.*

Daumier often used the conjugal bedroom to challenge the literary pretentiousness of the woman author. (See the series "Conjugal Manners.") She wears a prosaic negligee, and her husband's reflection is equally quotidian. To top it off he calls his wife "Bichette" (as in No. 29, L.D. 1236) at a time when women were giving each other names like Ismenie, Ophelia, Eudoxie, and Arsinoë. Note, too, the same candlelight as that used in No. 20.)

23. — TO THINK THAT ARSINOË WASN'T SATISFIED WITH HAVING HER PORTRAIT DONE, A DAGUERREOTYPE MADE OF HER, A LITHOGRAPH MADE OF HER, AND HER BIOGRA-PHY WRITTEN! . . . NOW I'VE GOT TO PAY THREE THOU-SAND FRANCS FOR A BUST OF HER IN MARBLE . . . IT'S TOUGH! . . . THE HARDEST PART IS THAT I HAVE TO DUST OFF MY WIFE EVERY MORNING . . . AND THIS WIFE OF MINE SURE MAKES A LOT OF DUST! . . .

L. Delteil, 1232, second of three artist's proofs. Plate 12 of the series. Published in *Le Charivari,* March 4, 1844.

This pensive husband standing before the marble bust of his wife should have meditated on the words of Saint-Beuve: "If you're searching for happiness in love, never love a muse. Where you believe you find her heart, you will only find talent."

"The story of the life of a Parisian woman is always the story of her mind, and never the story of her heart" (*Physiology of the Parisian Woman*). (See No. 3 for the type of woman portrayed here.)

24. — GOOD GRIEF! . . . HOW I WISH MY WIFE WOULD FINISH IMPROVISING HER QUATRAIN ON "THE BEAUTY OF NATURE IN THE FIELD OF SAINT DENIS"! . . . WE'RE STILL WALKING, BUT HER VERSES HAVEN'T MOVED A FOOT! . . .

L. Delteil, 1252, second of two artist's proofs. Plate 32 of the series published in *Le Charivari,* July 6, 1844.

It's impossible to think that Daumier didn't have in mind these lines from *Physiology of the Bluestocking* when he drew this plate. "Those are model husbands; those are in constant admiration of their adored spouses. When the wives honor them by going out in their company, these men walk behind them. If they're going by foot, they carry the umbrella, and in the event there are purchases made, they carry figurines, baskets of strawberries and pieces of cheese on their free arm." This plate and the two that follow are among the rare scenes in the series that are portrayed outdoors, rather than indoors.

25. — OH AGONY! . . . TO HAVE SPENT MY MAIDENHOOD DREAMING OF A HUSBAND WHO, LIKE ME, ADORED HALLOWED POETRY, AND TO WIND UP WITH A HUSBAND WHO ONLY LIKES TO BAIT GUDGEONS . . . THE MAN WAS BORN TO BE PIKED! . . .

L. Delteil, 1240, second of two artist's proofs. Plate 20 of the series. Published in *Le Charivari*, March 27, 1844.

Perhaps the novel this woman is holding in her hand is George Sand's *Corinne*: ". . . Sometimes I quote the most beautiful verses of various languages that I know. These divine verses that penetrate my soul are mine . . . when my soul is elevated, when it disdains egoism and baseness from on high . . . I feel like a poet . . . If I have to stifle my mind and spirit, of what use is it to keep the rest of life that troubles me to no avail."

Not only does this composition suggest the countryside, but it is also full of charm and poetry. The quality of the light shows a pre-Impressionist sensibility.

26. — OH VICTOR! MY IDOL! . . . I'VE JUST HAD A POETIC IDEA!! LET'S JUMP OFF THIS GRAY CLIFF TOGETHER INTO THE BLUE WAVES OF THE OCEAN, RIGHT NOW! . . .

— DROWN OURSELVES IN THE SEA?! . . . WE'LL THINK ABOUT IT, ANASTASIA . . . I'M STILL KEEN ON MOVING DOWN THE RIVER OF LIFE A WHILE LONGER! . . .

L. Delteil, 1238, second of two artist's proofs. Plate 18 of the series. Published in *Le Charivari*, March 19, 1844.

This is a far cry from women of humane or philosophical letters. It seems as if Daumier, who put a lot of poetry into his composition, has been touched somewhat by the romanticism of the woman's declaration. The same cliff that dominates the sea is also found in a lithograph of 1846 (L.D. 1489): "In heaven's name, Theodore, don't look at the sea like that. Something terrible will happen!" This time, however, it's the wife who keeps her husband from leaning what she considers to be too far over the cliff.

27. — THAT DOES IT! . . . THERE SHE GOES PUTTING BOOT POLISH INTO MY CHOCOLATE INSTEAD OF MILK! . . . DAMNED NOVEL, BLAST YOU! . . .

L. Delteil, 1257, second of two artist's proofs. Plate 37 of the series. Published in *Le Charivari*, July 29-30, 1844.

This plate, like those that follow, shows the Bluestocking neglecting her housework, her husband, and her children, or

refusing to be a slave in favor of reading a novel or writing her books.

28. — SINCE VIRGINIA OBTAINED THE SEVENTH HONORABLE MENTION IN POETRY AT THE FRENCH ACADEMY, IT'S ME . . . CAPTAIN OF THE NATIONAL GUARD . . . WHO HAS TO COUNT THE SHEETS EVERY SATURDAY BEFORE TAKING THEM TO THE LAUNDRESS . . . I DO IT BECAUSE IF I DIDN'T, MY WIFE WOULD HAUL ME OVER THE COALS! . . .

L. Delteil, 1244, second of three artist's proofs. Plate 24 of the series. Published in *Le Charivari*, April 18, 1844.

Physiology of the Bluestocking specifies that "married Bluestockings live with their husbands, don't live with their husbands, or, living with their husbands don't consider them husbands . . ." and with curiosity observes "just to what extent the head of the family was pushed in these strange households." Some husbands "adjusted marvelously to this annihilation, and willingly reduced themselves to the writing of a cookbook or to taking charge of the laundry . . ." There is in the same spirit a caricature by Gavarni that portrays *Monsieur à la cuisine, madame au piano*, "The man in the kitchen, the woman at the piano" (1843).

29. — BICHETTE . . . PLEASE COME AND ARRANGE MY TIE! . . .

— THAT'S MEN FOR YOU! . . . THEY ABUSE YOUR RIGHTS . . . JUST BECAUSE ONE DAY WE WERE WEAK ENOUGH TO TIE THE MARRIAGE KNOT WITH THEM, THEY EXPECT US TO ETERNALLY TIE THE KNOTS ON THEIR TIES! . . . BUT I'M DETERMINED HENCEFORTH TO FOLLOW THE PRINCIPLES ENUNCIATED BY ARTEMISE JAUTOT THIS VERY MORNING IN HER REMARKABLE ARTICLE IN *The Liberated Women's Gazette*: . . . "ABOLISH NECKTIES AND BUTTONS ON BREECHES!"

L. Delteil, 1236, second of three artist's proofs. Plate 16 of the series. Published in *Le Charivari*, March 13, 1844.

"Women must know that when they leave the care of their fathers, they enter into the care of their husbands . . . A husband must have absolute hegemony over the actions of his wife" (Napoleon). This was not the advice of either the Saint-Simonians, who felt that marriage should end as the first step toward a woman's complete liberation, or of George Sand, who demanded the equality of women in marriage. In the second preface to *Indiana* (1842), Sand appoints herself the apostle of women's rights: ". . . The war will be a long and hard one, but I'm neither the first, the last, nor the only champion of such a beautiful cause, and I will defend this cause until my last breath." The *Gazette des femmes libres*, "Liberated Women's Gazette," named in the caption is an allusion to the feminist political paper founded by Madame Herbinot de Mauchamps, the *Gazette des femmes*, "Women's Gazette" (1836-38). The articles encouraged women to "get out from under the masculine yoke." The end of the caption—"Abolish . . . buttons on breeches"— introduces the following plate.

30. — A WOMAN LIKE ME . . . SEW A BUTTON ON? . . .
YOU'RE MAD! . . .

— SO BE IT! . . . SO SHE NO LONGER IS SATISFIED
WEARING MY BREECHES . . . SHE HAS TO THROW THEM
ON MY HEAD! . . .

L. Delteil, 1248, second of three artist's proofs. Plate 28 of
the series. Published in *Le Charivari*, May 23, 1844.

The theme of the woman's refusal to perform the humiliating task of sewing on buttons was used many times by Daumier (see *Socialist Women*, No. 44). As early as 1838 *Le Charivari* had published a Daumier lithograph (L.D. 629) that portrayed a man asking his wife, who's sitting in a chair reading, to patch up his pants: "I don't give a damn about your Madame Sand who prevents women from patching up torn pants . . . They need to reinstate divorce . . . or eliminate that author" (see the series *Conjugal Manners*, No. 6).

The right to divorce, which had been instituted by the Constituent Assembly in 1789, was revoked in 1816. George Sand had fought hard to get it reinstated, and she wasn't alone in her fight. Flora Tristan, her contemporary and an ardent apostle of feminism, had petitioned unsuccessfully for its reinstatement in 1834. Her book *Pérégrination d'une paria*, "Peregrination of an Outcast" (1830), expressed her horror of marriage and justified divorce. Moreover, she demanded the general equality of women in society: "I am demanding rights for women because I am convinced that all the misery of the world issues from this disregard and disdain that has existed until now with regard to the natural and indefeasible rights of the female person . . ." (*Aux ouvriers et ouvrières*, "For Men and Women Laborers," extract from *L'Union ouvrière*, "The Workers' Union," " a journal for the rights, duties, and interests of all men and women").

The issue of divorce was a very current one. Daumier devoted to the subject the series *Divorceuses*, "Divorced Women" (L.D. 1769-74, six pieces that appeared between August and October 1848). It was very much in the spirit of *Bluestockings* and *Socialist Women*.

31. THE MOTHER IS IN THE HEAT OF WRITING. THE CHILD IS
IN THE BATH WATER!

L. Delteil, 1227, second of two artist's proofs. Plate 7 of the
series. Published in *Le Charivari*, February 26, 1844.

Stendhal, who favored the emancipation and education of women, considered it imprecise to say that a cultivated woman would not take care of her child if the child fell ill: "A young woman whose child has the measles would not be able . . . to take pleasure in reading Volney's *Travel to Syria* (Voyage en Syrié) any more than her rich banker husband could enjoy reading Malthus at the moment of bankruptcy. Stendhal adds that "allowing women perfect equality . . . would double the intellectual strength of the human race and its prospects for happiness." (Take note of the framed sketches on the wall, which seem to have real artistic value.)

32. — TAKE THAT AWAY FARTHER . . . IT'S IMPOSSIBLE TO
WORK IN THE MIDST OF SUCH A BROUHAHA. . . GO TAKE

A WALK ON THE OUTSKIRTS OF TOWN AND ON YOUR WAY
BACK BUY SOME MORE FORMULA ON CHOISEUL STREET!
. . . AH! MONSIEUR CABASSOL, THIS IS YOUR FIRST
CHILD, BUT I SWEAR TO YOU IT WILL BE YOUR LAST!

L. Delteil, 1231, second of two artist's proofs. Plate 11 of
the series. Published in *Le Charivari*, March 2, 1844.

"No one knows about the husband, unless a friend inquires as to how Madame's children are doing. They are told that the husband has gone for a stroll with them in Luxembourg Gardens" (*Physiology of the Bluestocking*). This theme was used several times by Daumier (see the two plates that follow), and had already been dealt with in the series *Moeurs Conjugales: Le Mari du bas-bleu*, "Conjugal Manners: The Bluestocking's Husband" (L.D. 669, 1842). The husband takes care of the children and makes sure that his wife is not disturbed: "My wife has been inspired since this morning" (*Conjugal Manners*, No. 46).

33. — OUT! YOU DISSOLUTE CHILD FROM HELL! . . . LET
ME COMPOSE MY ODE TO THE JOY OF MOTHERHOOD *in
peace*! . . .

— IT'S OKAY, IT'S OKAY . . . HE'LL BE QUIET! . . . I'M
GOING TO GIVE HIM THE STRAP IN THE OTHER ROOM . . .
[ASIDE] THE FACT IS, THAT OF ALL MY WIFE'S
"WORKS," THIS KID STIRS UP THE MOST COMMOTION IN
SOCIETY! . . .

L. Delteil, 1231, second of three artist's proofs. Plate 14 of
the series. Published in *Le Charivari*, March 2, 1844.

"Marriage is a yoke for all women. It's a prison for certain Bluestockings, who never enter it without first arming themselves with a pen and quill . . ." (*Physiology of the Bluestocking*). *The Regional Muse* and *Madame Bovary* make allusions to the bad influence that reading George Sand had on women: ". . . that sentimental leprosy which has been the ruin of so many women who, without their pretension to genius, could otherwise have been charming . . . The example set by George Sand had the principal effect of making it known that France possesses an exorbitant number of superior women." (Balzac, *The Regional Muse*).

34. — GOOD-BYE, MY DEAR. I'M GOING TO SEE MY PUBLISHERS . . . I PROBABLY WON'T BE BACK UNTIL VERY LATE . . .
DON'T FORGET TO GIVE LITTLE DODORE ANOTHER TWO
FEEDINGS OF PAP . . . IF HE NEEDS . . . SOMETHING ELSE
. . . YOU'LL FIND THAT UNDER THE BED . . .

L. Delteil, 1223, second of three artist's proofs. Plate 3 of
the series. Published in *Le Charivari*, February 8, 1844.

Daumier's sketch pencil meets again the sarcasm of *Physiology of the Bluestocking* to express indignation against this nonconformist situation. While the husband stays at home with the children, ". . . Madame goes out at night, and Madame has a meeting in the morning; Madame is with her bookseller; Madame is with her printer . . ."

According to Leon Abensour, the reason public opinion is so hostile to all ideas regarding the emancipation of women is that "France is accustomed to considering feminism, which it saw emerge during the hours of the Revolution, as an endangerment to the solidity of family values and the salvation of the Nation . . . and, for many years, all apostles of the emancipation of women were up against the same indignation and the same sarcasm" (*Histoire générale du feminisme, des origines à nos jours,* "General History of Feminism from its Origins to the Present," 1921).

35. — CAN I COME IN, MY DEAR FRIEND? . . . HAVE YOU FINISHED COLLABORATING WITH THE GENTLEMAN? . . .

L. Delteil, 1249, second of two artist's proofs. Plate 29 of the series. Published in *Le Charivari,* May 30, 1844.

Daumier dedicated many caricatures to the Bluestocking and her collaborator. A passage from *Physiology of the Bluestocking* seems to have been truly useful to him as a point of departure for this lithograph: "I was going to the home of a Bluestocking for one or another matter; the husband arrived at the same moment I did. I asked if he would tell her I was there, and he offered to check and see if his wife was available; then he returned to tell me that she was in a meeting with M—."

36. — WHAT DO YOU SAY, DEAR HUSBAND? . . . I REALLY FEEL LIKE CALLING MY NEW DRAMA *Arthur* AND TITLING MY CHILD *Oscar*! . . . BUT OF COURSE NOT . . . UPON THINKING ABOUT IT, I WON'T MAKE ANY DECISIONS BEFORE CONSULTING MY COLLABORATOR! . . .

L. Delteil, 1222, second of three artist's proofs. Plate 2 of the series. Published in *Le Charivari,* February 1, 1844.

Father Enfantin stated that it was "the woman's decision to judge whether or not it was suitable for the child to know his or her father." This sort of statement was nothing more than theory, because in reality women didn't have that much clout in the hierarchy of the Saint-Simonians.

37. — IT'S QUITE SINGULAR . . . LATELY I'VE BEEN GETTING MORE IDEAS WHEN I TROT THROUGH THE BOIS DE BOULOGNE WITH MONSIEUR EDOUARD! . . .
— WHAT IDEAS COULD POSSIBLY ENTER MY WIFE'S HEAD WHILE SHE'S TROTTING WITH MONSIEUR EDOUARD? . . . THIS INTRIGUES ME. I'M ANGRY TO SEE THAT SHE'S MADE HERSELF INTO A HORSEWOMAN . . . I WOULD HAVE PREFERRED SHE SIMPLY STAY IN THE SADDLE OF VIRTUE! . . .

L. Delteil, 1247, second of two artist's proofs. Plate 27 of the series. Published in *Le Charivari,* May 12, 1844.

A variation on the theme of collaboration (see No. 35).

38. — OH DARLING! WHAT IS THIS SINGULAR EDUCATION YOU'RE GIVING TO YOUR DAUGHTER? . . . WHEN I WAS TWELVE YEARS OLD, I HAD ALREADY FINISHED A TWO-VOLUME NOVEL . . . AND AFTER I FINISHED IT, MY MOTHER EVEN FORBADE ME TO READ IT, BECAUSE SHE FOUND IT TOO ADVANCED FOR A GIRL OF MY AGE . . .

L. Delteil, 1255, second of two artist's proofs. Plate 35 of the series. Published in *Le Charivari,* July 20, 1844.

This little girl makes one think of Chardin's *Benedicité,* or maybe Balzac's *Eugénie Grandet* (1833), who spends long hours on a small chair next to her mother. "For the past fifteen years, the mother and daughter have peacefully spent each day working endlessly in this place," maintaining the house linens and embroidering (*Les Petites Filles modèles,* "Exemplary Young Girls," 1858).

39. ". . . WERE THEY TO CURSE ME,
"THESE BARBAROUS PARENTS WHO GAVE BIRTH TO ME,
"O VICTOR, O MY SOUL! ALL MY LOVE IS FOR YOU!"
— BRAVO . . . BRAVO . . . BRAVO . . . HOW HAPPY FOR A MOTHER TO HAVE SUCH A LITTLE DAUGHTER! . . .

L. Delteil, 1256, second of two artist's proofs. Plate 36 of the series. Published in *Le Charivari,* July 26, 1844.

Daumier takes a different approach to one of the ideas he so favored — that of the "greetings" bestowed on Parents' Day or on New Year's Day (see, for example, L.D. 627). He wasn't the only one to mock this ritual: "The children arrive with their greetings written by their schoolmaster . . . and recite the insipid banalities for the occasion that they were taught just like parrots" (L. Couailhac, *Physiologie du Jour de l'an,* "Physiology of New Year's Day," drawings by Henri Emy). In *Madame Bovary* Emma shows her future husband the drawings she did as a child: "To decorate the apartment there was the head of Athena in black crayon which was framed in gold and hung on the wall by a nail. At the bottom of the frame were Gothic letters that read: To My Papa."

40. I'LL BE! ANOTHER CARICATURE OF US IN THIS MORNING'S *Charivari*! . . . AH! MY WORD! I CERTAINLY HOPE THAT THIS TIME IT WILL BE THE LAST! . . . AND IF DAUMIER EVER CROSSES MY PATH, HE'LL PAY DEARLY FOR HAVING TAKEN UPON HIMSELF THE LIBERTY TO KNIT HIS BLUESTOCKINGS.

L. Delteil, 1259, second of two artist's proofs. Plate 39 of the series. Published in *Le Charivari,* August 3, 1844.

Daumier gave this scene — the second-to-last in the series —a rather theatrical aspect: the agitated staging, the contrast of the white dress with the black, the vehement anger expressed by the two Bluestockings, one of whom evokes the image described in *Physiology of the Bluestocking,* with "her hair full of tragedy and melancholy thoughts." Daumier often relied on word-play to convey the comic dimension of the captions, and enjoyed interjecting himself at times into them. For example, when the Bluestockings were pretentious enough to consider themselves writers, he, on the other hand, "knitted."

SOCIALIST WOMEN.

A series of ten plates numbered from 1 to 10 and published in *Le Charivari* from April to June 1849. L. Delteil, 1918 to 1927.

41. INSURRECTION AGAINST HUSBANDS IS PROCLAIMED THE HIGHEST OF OBLIGATIONS!

L. Delteil, 1918, second of two artist's proofs. Plate 1 of the series. Published in *Le Charivari*, April 20, 1849.

"Socialist women [sic] gathered together . . . to proclaim the abolition of husbands." This was *Le Charivari's* (April 25, 1849) commentary on the new play *Socialist Women*, presented at the Montansier Theater. It was a one-act vaudeville show by Messrs. Varin and Roger de Beauvoir. "It seems that the Montansier Theater is in competition with *Le Charivari*; we accept the challenge! Cham and Daumier will stand up to Varin and Roger de Beauvoir . . . This vaudeville will be a stream of extravagances . . . Disputes, self-proclaimed heroines, victories, hair-pulling; to sum it up: the faithful depiction of a real-life women's club. The jokes are perhaps a bit bold, but when it comes to Socialist women, nothing is too daring . . ." In 1848, *La Republique des femmes*, "The Women's Republic," published a small rebellious couplet against the masculine stranglehold:

> Forward and on! Let us free the earth
> Of tyrants that for too long have stood!
> Let's wage war against the beards . . .

Numerous satirical pieces in the same vein appeared in 1848. For example: an "illustrated song" titled *La Marseillaise des femmes*, "The Women's Marseillaise"; *Le Chant du départ de ces dames, ou grande expédition contre ces gueux de maris*, "The Ladies' Farewell Song, or The Great Expedition Against These Beggarly Husbands" (June 1848); *Le Chant des citoyennes*, "Song of Women Citizens"; and "Arise Women, Progress Is Calling You" (Bibliothèque Nationale, the Vinck Print Collection).

42. — AH! HE'S TRYING TO KEEP ME FROM JOINING OUR EIGHT HUNDRED BROTHERS AT THE BARRIER ON AVENUE DU MAINE . . . THIS INSOLENCE MUST BE PUNISHED!
— CALM DOWN, ÉGLANTINE. LEAVE THIS TYRANT TO THE REMORSE OF HIS CONSCIENCE.

L. Delteil, 1921, second of two artist's proofs. Plate 4 of the series. Published in *Le Charivari*, May 7, 1849.

"You said: 'Private life is the only one suitable for a woman; she is not at all made for public life . . . Life is threefold in its unity: private life, family life, and social life makes for a full life.' I say: 'Grant women the right to a social life; to refuse her this aspect of life is a treasonous crime against humanity'" (Jeanne Derouin, "Letter from a Woman to Monsieur Athanase Coquerel," August 1848). Coquerel was the chairman of the committee that drafted the decree ordering the closing of the

women's clubs (see No. 47), an act that provoked the vehement protest of Jeanne Derouin. During a meeting of a women's club, one of the citizens let her indignation fly: "Must I remain forever bound by law to a tyrant who takes egotism to the extreme and absolutism to the point of forbidding me to come to this club? But . . . I overrode his protests and I came here as a woman who knows her rights and wants to have them respected."

The barrier in question was situated at the spot where avenue du Maine intersected the wall of the Farmers-General (at the junction of boulevard Edgar Quinet and boulevard de Vaugirard). Leroux had built two amusement pavilions connected by a wire fence, and the array of cabarets and refreshment stands attracted a broad and diverse public: *La Californie*, "The California," and *Le Bal Tonnelier*, "The Cooper's Ball," with its salon that "could accommodate 200 diners at a sitting" (J. Hillairet, *Historical Dictionary of the Paris Streets*). A "rendezvous for drinkers and ragpickers," the cabarets were "also frequented by writers and artists" (Labedollière).

43. — OH! SO YOU'RE MY HUSBAND! HMM! SO *you're* THE MASTER OF THIS HOUSE . . . WELL! IT'S MY RIGHT TO THROW YOU OUT THE DOOR OF YOUR OWN HOUSE . . . JEANNE DEROUIN PROVED IT TO ME LAST NIGHT! . . . SO GO DISCUSS THIS WITH HER! . . .

L. Delteil, 1924, second of two artist's proofs. Plate 7 of the series. Published in *Le Charivari*, May 23, 1849.

Again we see depicted the revolt against the husband's authority that tickled Daumier's wit. The speeches Jeanne Derouin gave with courage and conviction seem full of measure and conviction when we read them today. In her time, however, they were considered subversive and created a scandal: "We affirm that women have the same right to liberty, equality, and fraternity as men. Equality means the same for a woman as it does for a man—the right and the duty to participate in all the acts of social life according to his or her abilities and aptitudes . . . Humanity is composed of women and men . . . The political liberty of women is the first step toward freedom for all those who are oppressed" (Jeanne Derouin, *Association fraternelle des démocrates socialistes des deux sexes, pour l'affranchissement politique et social des femmes*, "The Fraternal Association of Democratic-Socialists of Both Sexes for the Political Liberation of Women," 1849).

44. — YES, MY DEAR. MY HUSBAND ASSAULTED MY DIGNITY AS A WOMAN TO THE POINT OF FORCING ME THIS VERY MORNING TO SEW A BUTTON ON HIS BREECHES! . . .
— MY HEAVENS, IF A MAN FORCED ME TO WORK ON HIS BREECHES! . . .

L. Delteil, 1922, second of two artist's proofs. Plate 5 of the series. Published in *Le Charivari*, May 11, 1849.

Daumier has already dealt with this theme many times. See *Bluestockings*, No. 30.

45. — MY, MY . . . WHY ARE YOU GETTING ALL DOLLED UP, MY DEAR! . . .

— AH! IT'S BECAUSE I'M GOING TO A BANQUET WHERE PIERRE LEROUX IS OFFICIATING ... AND IF YOU KNEW HOW FINICKY HE IS ABOUT PROPER DRESS! ...

L. Delteil, 1919, second of two artist's proofs. Plate 2 of the series. Published in *Le Charivari*, April 23, 1849.

At the end of 1848 and the beginning of 1849, socialist banquets, especially for women, occurred quite frequently. Two in particular seem to have been rather important: the Regenerative Banquet of Democratic and Socialist Women, which took place on November 25, 1848, at the Dunoyer Restaurant at the avenue du Maine barrier and was presided over by Pierre Leroux, Bernard, and Armand Barbès; and one that took place on Christmas Day of the same year and was presided over by Leroux and Felix Pyat. Leroux, a Socialist and partisan of Saint-Simonism, fought strongly in favor of the emancipation of women. In 1851, he went so far as to demand the right for women to vote in the municipal elections. His efforts did not, however, meet with success.

Daumier emphasized the theme of the alleged physical unattractiveness of women who involved themselves in literature or socialism. A plate published on January 25, 1849 (L.D. 1794), is very much in the spirit of this one. "To think that Proudhon doesn't want us to go to the socialist banquets, ... The poor man has therefore never known what it is to love, ... He's ignoring the fact that a woman's presence embellishes everything!"

46. — MY WIFE HAS BEEN AT THAT BANQUET FOR AN AWFULLY LONG TIME ... SHE LEFT HERE ALMOST FORTY-EIGHT HOURS AGO! ...

L. Delteil, 1927, second of two artist's proofs. Plate 10 of the series. Published in *Le Charivari*, June 9, 1849.

Here Daumier deals with three themes: Socialist women's banquets, husbands who have been left at home to take care of the child, and the wife's infidelity. The latter two were often the subject matter of the *Bluestockings* series.

47. — IT SEEMS THAT THE CLUBS ARE GOING TO BE COMPLETELY CLOSED DOWN ...

— THOSE REACTIONARIES ... THEY WOULD NEVER HAVE DARED DO THAT BEFORE THE LEGION OF VESUVIANS WAS DISSOLVED! ...

L. Delteil, 1920, second of two artist's proofs, Plate 3 of the series. Published in *Le Charivari*, April 25, 1849.

Following the Revolution of 1848, hundreds of clubs opened; records show that more than 300 of them existed in March of that year. A number of feminist clubs also came into being, the most important of which are described here.

The Women's Club was founded by Eugénie Niboyet, who for many years had been a leader in the women's liberation movement. Her publication, *La Voix des femmes*, "Women's Voice," was published from March 20 to June 20, 1848. The club and newspaper depended on the Society of Women's Voices, which fast became a primary force in the feminist movement.

Another important group, which had a distinctly more political character, was the Club for the Emancipation of Women, founded by Jeanne Derouin, Desirée Gay, and Dr. Malatier. They had proposed the publication of a newspaper titled *Women's Tribune*, but it never materialized due to lack of funds. Gay had founded the newspaper *La Politique des femmes*, "Women's Politics," of which only two issues were published. The journal founded by Derouin, *L'Opinion des femmes*, "Women's Opinion," published six issues in the course of one year, owing its fame to both the personality of Jeanne Derouin and the writings of Jean Mace. The Committee for Women's Rights was another very political club.

The women's clubs had numerous problems. On April 19, 1848, the government issued a proclamation "requesting that the women's clubs curb their ardent patriotism" (M. de Villiers, *Histoire des clubs de femmes*, "History of Women's Clubs," 1910). On July 26 a new law was put before the National Assembly that led to the decree of July 28, which stipulated in Article 3 that "women and children who are not of legal age cannot be members in clubs or attend meetings." This law provoked many indignant protests and led Derouin to write a letter to Athanase Coquerel (see No. 42). Charles Hugo, in an article that appeared in Liberty (May 29, 1848), was equally harsh with regard to women's clubs: "I have never been to this club and have no intention of ever doing so ... The only thing to be seen there is a red bonnet on a Bluestocking." In January 1849, the matter escalated to the proposed abolition of all existing clubs. The law was voted into effect on March 20.

The Vesuvians, a group alluded to in the caption, was an organization of women who banded together to improve their lot and fight for the emancipation of women. "They were believers in the total community" and were "emblazoned to the depths of their being with revolutionary ardor" (Leon Abensour, *Histoire ... du feminisme*, "History of Feminism," 1921). However, they were best known for the eccentricities of their dress and behavior. Their clothes were masculine, almost military. Citizen Borme's proposal for the creation of a "national guard of women" provided ample satirical fodder for months to come. Edouard de Beaumont, in particular, devoted an entire eighteen plates to a series that appeared in *Le Charivari* between May and November 1848 (see the catalogue of the Vinck Print Collection, Nos. 14136-153). Ultimately this group did more harm than good for the women's movement, due to the extent of criticism elicited.

48. "... WHAT IS A WOMAN IN TODAY'S SOCIETY? NOTHING! WHAT MUST SHE BE? EVERYTHING! ..."

— OH! BRAVO, BRAVO! THAT EVEN MORE BEAUTIFUL THAN THE LAST DISCOURSE BY JEANNE DEROUIN! ...

L. Delteil, 1923, second of two artist's proofs. Plate 6 of the series. Published in *Le Charivari*, May 17, 1849.

In *L'Éducation Sentimentale*, "A Sentimental Education" (ed. Dumesnil, 2:124), Flaubert traces a portrait of Vatnaz that seems close in inspiration to the one on this plate:

She was one of those single Parisians, who . . . dream of love, a family, a hearth and fortune, all that is absent in their lives. Like many others, these women welcomed the arrival of the time for revenge that the Revolution brought with it. They threw themselves into unbridled socialist propaganda. According to Vatnaz the liberation of the proletariat was possible only on the condition that the liberation of women occurred. She wanted women to be eligible for all types of work, the paternal quest, . . . "a more intelligent marriage routine." Thus, every French woman would be obliged to marry a Frenchman or to adopt an old man . . . And since the government was unaware and lacked knowledge of their rights, they would have to use force to fight force. Ten thousand well-armed female citizens could bring down City Hall.

Jeanne Derouin, who at this time was incontestably the most colorful, original, and active militant on the scene, demanded in her journal *Women's Opinion* the abolition of all privileges related to race, birth, fortune, and gender. She gave courses in general history and in social rights for women. The following is from her *Cours de droit social pour les femmes*, "Course on Social Rights for Women" (1848):

Humanity moves forward and increases in time and space, but women, however, remain enslaved, and violated in silence, . . . they are subjugated under the yoke of men . . . Great social reform is called for. It is necessary and inevitable; but in order for this reform to be total and enduring, it must come from men alone. Men only know how to establish order by despotism; women only know how to organize through the strength of their maternal love. Both are needed in order to conciliate order and freedom. Oh Women! . . . rise up and speak out in the name of humanity! It is God who commands this: it is more than a right. It is an obligation.

49. "THE DELEGATES TO THE CENTRAL SOCIALIST CLUB UNANIMOUSLY REJECTED THE CANDIDACY OF JEANNE DEROUIN!"

— OH! THOSE ARISTOCRATS! . . .

L. Delteil, 1925, second of two artist's proofs. Plate 8 of the series. Published in *Le Charivari*, May 25, 1849.

In April 1849, Jeanne Derouin proposed her candidacy for a seat in the National Assembly. "Too intelligent to anticipate her success, she at least wanted to attract attention to the idea of feminism with a stunning demonstration. This was at the beginning of a reactionary period, and she was well aware that the movement was already fading into general indifference" (Leon Abensour, *History . . . of feminism*). Her candidacy

caused a scandal. Proudhon wrote in his newspaper *Le Peuple:* "We no better understand a woman legislator than we do a male wet-nurse." He forcefully affirmed that "a woman's place is in the home; a man's place is in society."

50. — THRUST ASIDE AS A CANDIDATE TO THE NATIONAL ASSEMBLY, I FIND STILL ONE DOOR OPEN TO ME . . . LEAVE ME ALONE, ZENOBIE . . . DON'T INTERRUPT MY THOUGHT PROCESS . . . I'M IN THE MIDST OF DRAFTING A MANIFESTO TO EUROPE! . . .

L. Delteil, 1926, second of two artist's proofs. Plate 9 of the series. Published in *Le Charivari*, June 4, 1849.

The series *Socialist Women* ended soon after the elections of May 13. Though Jeanne Derouin received only about fifteen votes, she continued nonetheless to campaign for the feminist cause. On May 29, 1850, she and seven other women, along with many men, were arrested during a meeting. Derouin and Madame Pauline Roland were sentenced to six months in prison. In 1853, Derouin was living in exile in London, from where she published *The Women's Almanac for 1853*. In it is the "Discourse given by Victor Hugo on the tomb of Louise Julien, banished to Jersey where she died in 1853," which ends with the following passage:

. . . The eighteenth century proclaimed the rights of man; the nineteenth century will proclaim the rights of women; — but citizens, we must admit that we haven't rushed to this; many serious decisions, I agree, that had to be fully examined, slowed us down; and at this very moment, the very moment when this progress was arrived at, among the best Republicans, among the truest and purest of Democrats, many fine minds are still hesitating to admit the equality in men and women of the human soul, and consequently the assimilation, not to mention the complete identity of civil rights. Let us say it loud and clear, citizens, that as long as prosperity has lasted, as long as the Republic has been in place, women have been forgotten by us.

The feminist movement born with the Revolution of 1848 also died with it. Public opinion was still impregnated with the spirit that had dominated the writing of the Civil Code, and the general public had barely paid any attention to the feminist movement — except for its most spectacular manifestations, which often least merited interest. Nonetheless, "how many new feminist ideas there were! . . . They seemed utopian then, if not ridiculous" (Leon Abensour, *History . . . of feminism*). Today we consider them the precursors of the movement. Not one of the fundamental demands of contemporary feminism was omitted. They paved the path for future reforms.